Working in a Team

A workbook to successful dynamics

Note
Health care practice and knowledge are constantly changing and developing as new research and treatments, changes in procedures, drugs and equipment become available.

The author and publishers have, as far as is reasonably possible, taken care to confirm that the information complies with the latest standards of practice and legislation.

Working in a Team

A workbook to successful dynamics

by

Jean Bayliss

QUAY
BOOKS

A division of MA Healthcare Ltd

Quay Books Division, MA Healthcare Ltd, St Jude's Church, Dulwich Road, London SE24 0PB

British Library Cataloguing-in-Publication Data
A catalogue record is available for this book

© MA Healthcare Limited 2009
ISBN-10: 1-85642-368-9
ISBN-13: 978-1-85642-368-7

Printed in the UK by CLE, St Ives, Cambridgeshire

Contents

Introduction

Most readers of this book will have been members of a group; some will be, or are, members of a team. Many of the dynamics which exist in groups are replicated in teams, yet there are important and significant differences. For example, we can often choose the group to which we belong but we may have little choice about the team to which we are assigned for our work.

Healthcare is arguably one the area which requires effective team work: its mission is to provide effective clinical and holistic care and no single person, however devoted and expert, can meet the diversity of challenge. The needs of a patient and of those closest to him or her are infinitely varied and diverse, and similar variety and diversity is called for in the care offered to them. Effective team work is not just a priority in healthcare — it is an imperative.

The word 'dynamics' comes from the Greek word 'force' and it is with this in mind that this book considers team dynamics, in the sense that the dynamics in a team arc a powerful force for enhancing care and for rewarding team members for meeting the challenges the work presents, work which can be physically, emotionally and spiritually demanding. The support and encouragement of others who share the health care vision can be very sustaining. Effective teams show a willingness to work together to a common plan; in our case to provide excellence in care. Members work interdependently and are mutually supportive. The efforts of a team are several times more than the efforts individuals could achieve if they were to work independently. An analogy might be an orchestra, where a performance of a great work is more than the individual sounds of each instrument, however well played. The energy released when people work effectively in a team can transform whole organisations.

This book aims to offer insight into what makes teams work. Because team work is interactive, its style is also interactive. In this text you are offered the opportunity to reflect on various points as you proceed, and spaces are left for you to write your comments if you wish, or you might prefer to keep a reflective journal. Whether you are a team leader or a team member reflecting on your role and contribution to your care team will help to bring the insight which is critical for the care provided.

Good teams display high levels of motivation, and enthusiasm and energy for the work, its members are fired up with enthusiasm and with both physical and mental energy and are creative about the interventions provided for patients and those closest to them. Moreover, they model their care for patients by supporting and caring for each other. How could this mutuality not benefit patients? Who would not want to be part of such a dynamic force?

V. Jean Bayliss
MA (Counselling), BA (Hons.); Postgraduate Diploma (Counselling in Educational Settings), Dip. Life Coaching;,Fellow Charted Institute of Educational Assessors.

CHAPTER I

What is a team?

Terms such as 'team player' and 'team work' are frequently used in a health care context, and it is arguably this area where effective team work is most vital. The value of effective team work seems to be widely recognised. Most management text books have one or more sections on team building, team development, team management, etc. There seems to be a consensus that collective working helps to make the most of human resources.

'Human resources' is a term used to describe the individuals who make up a team, and perhaps the term highlights the tensions that can affect, for good or bad, the effectiveness of a team. A team is not a 'resource' in the way that the various parts of a machine or a mechanical process might be; it is made up of people (as opposed to parts), with individual strengths and aspirations who can make varied contributions to the team. A team approach in care is important because it is such a multi-faceted discipline, requiring an equally wide range of expertise. The team approach emphasises collective working methods and responsibilities, but at the same time encourages individual expertise and experience. Being a part of, living with and managing the dynamics of such a complex entity is not easy, and team membership itself can present a discipline which is difficult for some members.

The word 'team' is very widely used in everyday life, especially of course in sport. Indeed sport might offer a very useful analogy for the ways in which diverse positions are equally essential for the whole: in a winning team the success is dependent upon each player knowing what part to play and when, and even thought there may be only one goal scorer there is equality of contribution.

Despite its very common use, it is not always clear what is meant by 'team' and attempting some kind of definition of what we think a team actually is may be helpful. Take a moment to attempt your personal definition of a team, particularly in relation to health care (see *Box 1*).

In a definition of 'team' a dictionary definition would include words such as collaborate, co-operate, team spirit. (It might also include words like clannish or elitist!) Useful though a definition might be, it does not seem fully to explain what makes a team work or what makes good teams effective (see *Box 2*).

Below are six characteristics which have been suggested as features which define a team. As you read each one, try to decide whether it is true for the palliative care team of which you are a member. These six characteristics were contributed by a team of palliative care workers, which included professionals and volunteers, but they are applicable to any healthcare team.

Think box 1

Write down your own definition of what is a team.

Think box 2

Write down what components a team should have.

---

1. **The members are identifiable by the name of the team to which they belong.**

    'It's quite nice to be able to say "I work for *** ". It gives me a bit of a boost.'

    'At least it lets people know what line of work you're in.'

    'It works quite well if people know you belong to ***, but occasionally it can work against you if people don't know much about ***, or even have negative feelings about us.'

    'It's something to be proud of; but if you belonged to some teams you might want to hide it'.

2. **The members actually see themselves as a group, they have a conscious sense of being part of a collective operation or process, they identify with other members and acknowledge individual contributions (their own and those of others).**

    'I have mixed feelings about this: I am aware that I'm part of a team, but sometimes, because I'm not usually at base, I feel a bit of an outsider.'

    'It's a problem. So many of us are in and out of ***, and I don't think I really know half of the team.'

    'Yes! It's great, because I can identify with other team members because we're all subject to the same stresses and strains.'

3. **There is a sense of common goals or tasks. In heath care this should
    be something related to ensuring the best care for a patient and those
    closest to him or her up to and after the death.**

    'Oh definitely.'

    'Yes, patients and families first, every time.'

    'Well there wouldn't be any point otherwise'.

4. **There is an acknowledgement that members need the help of one another to
    accomplish the overall goal or aim. In health care an example might be that
    a nurse providing physical care and comfort for a patient might need the
    help of the team's social worker to obtain welfare benefits for the family.**

    *'Palliative care is so complex that one person couldn't cover everything; it's not
    like some specialist services, even though it is a specialism.'*

    'I'd be lost if I couldn't have help from the others.'

    *'Some of the cases I've faced are just too much. Sometimes I just don't have the
    knowledge or the expertise. I really need the others and so do the patients.'*

5. **The members communicate with each other, react to each other, and they
    may influence each other. There is an awareness that they are responsible
    to and for each other. This may be the most difficult area to accommodate,
    given the complexity of individual contributions within a health care team.**

    *'I suppose we do communicate in the core team, but I don't know many of the
    volunteers even though they're essential to some of "my" patients and to our
    service in general.'*

    'Meetings are good as you get different perspectives. Case discussion is good too.'

    *'To be honest perhaps I'm not a team player. I don't feel the need to interact
    in a general way and sometimes it seems a bit of a waste time, when I could
    be with the patients.'*

    'Interacting has a had a profound effect, for the better, on my practice.'

6. The team should be capable of working as a single unit. It is this characteristic which can reveal the strengths or weaknesses of a team and is where the dynamics are most evident.

'Well, yes, everything *** does should show the same patient care.'

'I don't know perhaps ACT is the crucial word? We have to be seen as one, but it's important that it doesn't mean papering over the cracks when there are real differences.'

'Sort of there are a lot of sub-groups.'

'When it comes to the crunch, we do all pull together.'

Think Box 3

What are your reactions?
Would your responses be at all similar in relation to your own team?
Did any of the responses resonate with you or surprise you?

What are your reactions to these comments? Would your responses be at all similar in relation to your own team? Did any of the responses resonate with you or surprise you? Write your thoughts in *Box 3*.

An important aspect of a health care team is that the skills, knowledge, expertise and experience of team members should be complementary. A team with a poor 'mix' of expertise would be very unbalanced and this would affect (probably adversely) the team dynamics.

Try to draw a diagram of the mixture of expertise in your team as in the example opposite. Is there a complementary balance? A crucial factor in any team's effectiveness is that it can benefit from the distinctive talents each member brings and simultaneously utilise these constructively. This is not likely to be the result of an unbalanced team and can lead to unhealthy competitiveness. You will have heard the expressions '*the whole should be greater than the sum of its parts*', and '*one weak link and the whole chain snaps*'. The first expression seems a worthwhile aim for a team — all the talents added together make an entity that is more than the collection itself. The second expression may perhaps act as a warning? It may be possible to create a perfectly balanced team in terms of skills, knowledge, experience, but, as well as knowing that they are team members who have a common purpose, a team needs individuals who have shared values. It is the shared values and insight into these which underpin good effective teams, and this depends as much on personalities as on expertise. The dynamics between individuals can make or mar team effectiveness.

Figure 1. An example of a representation of the of mixture of expertise in a palliative care team. Within other areas of health care the different levels of expertise may vary depending on its scope or its location..

Function

A further way of defining what makes a team is to consider its functions — what teams actually do — and how they can benefit an organisation. We can look at function in terms of the positive contributions a team and team work can make to the overall effectiveness of a health care service.

Induction

Teams are not static, fixed groups: the personnel can change and the skills mix vary, but if the team is a coherent and defined group, it can accept and absorb new members and ensure that values and priorities are maintained. It can be strong enough to manage internal transitions and changes. The team function is to model good transition.

Creativity

Interaction between team members generates, fosters and evaluates new thinking. Fresh thinking is more likely to come from a team than from solo working. Innovation thrives on interaction.

Coordination

The complexity of health care tasks requires similar complexity of expertise. A good team contributes to the coordination of this complexity, which would be unlikely if left to one person alone.

Decision-making

In health care there is a need for sound strategic thinking. Strategic decisions have great significance, not least for financial resources. Within the hospital setting decisions are also subject to pressures from inside as well as outside the organisation. All providers are aware that they may have to compete in order to ensure survival. There are also decisions about the quality of patient care and the difficulties involved in deciding criteria for what makes for more than 'good enough' care and what demonstrates excellence. There may be decisions as to which area of expertise should or should not benefit at any one time from what may well be limited resources .

A team contribution to decision-making can have important advantages. A range of different options and outcomes can be discussed and debated and, if this is well managed, a collective decision can be reached. People are more likely to be committed to decisions in which they have been involved, even if the decision is not one they are wholly satisfied with. The collective nature of the decision is more likely to achieve a consensus way of working and ensure the model of loyalty and coherence which we know patients and clients value.

Support

A consciousness that the team as individuals and as an entity need support is critical for effective working. This mutuality can contribute to the overall physical and psychological health of the service and will benefit service users as well as team members.

From time to time, it is helpful for a team to give itself, so to speak a 'health check'. As a final exercise for this chapter, give your team a rating (of between 1 and 6, 1 being worst and 6 being best) against the criteria set out in *Box 4* opposite. Think if there is other criteria that you would want to include.

Belbin RM (1981) *Management teams — Why they succeed or fail.* Heinemann, London

Think Box 4

Give your team a rating of between 1 (lowest) and 6 (highest) against the following criteria. Following this reflect on whether your scores truly reflect how effective your health care team is.

	1	2	3	4	5	6
Is there a good balance of expertise within your team?						
How clear is your team about what it wants to achieve?						
Do team members trust each other?						
Can your team confront issues and deal with them in an open way?						
Does the team have sound procedures for decision-making?						
Is the team able to use both cooperation and conflict to reach decisions?						
Is your team led in a way which helps the task, the team and individual members?						
Are there sufficient opportunities to review how the team is working?						
Are individuals within the team able to develop?						
How well does your team relate to other teams?						

CHAPTER 2

Models of team 'life'

There seems to be a general agreement that for most organisations and institutions teams are a 'good thing', but of course the value of a team is measured by its outcomes or its effectiveness. Poor team performance can be a source of stress and unhappiness for individual members and eventually outcomes will suffer. In the health care setting this can mean that the quality of the service declines to perhaps 'good enough' instead of 'excellent'.

Social psychologists have attempted to determine how teams develop and function, and some insight into their research findings and the models they suggest can be helpful in determining the strengths and weaknesses of a team. One of the best known models of the 'life' of a team is that of Tuckman and Jensen (1965). Their findings as to how teams form and develop suggest a set of stages, which could be represented as in *Figure 1*:

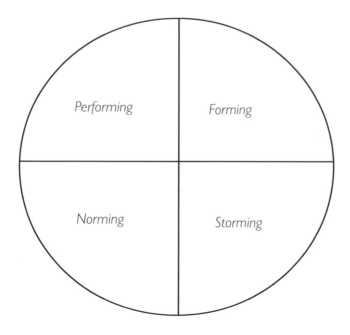

Figure 1. Tuckman and Jensen's (1965) model of the 'life' of a team.

Tuckman and Jensen (1965) argue that irrespective of their make-up (the individuals in the team) and of their overt task, teams develop in the same way and move through the same stages. The length of time taken to move through the phases will depend upon the individuals, their reasons for being in the team, the contribution(s) they make. Whether the team is new, 'from scratch' so to speak, or whether it is less fixed and incorporates new members as people leave is also a factor.

Forming

The forming stage occurs before individuals really see themselves as a team, even though they may have an identifiable name. The characteristic behaviours of members at this stage is that they are polite, impersonal, watchful and guarded. Individuals are likely to be asking themselves: *'What am I doing here?'*, *'Do I really belong here?'*. They may also be wondering the same sort of thing about others, especially if they have not met them before, or even if they have.

If no efforts are made to help members define their objectives and gain some sense of group identity this phase can continue indefinitely, and although some tasks may be tackled and completed the main process task, that of becoming a team, is never achieved.

Team members describe this first stage of development as very difficult, even if they have belonged to teams within the same organisation previously.

I asked a group of nurses who were brought together to devise a curriculum to record their initial feelings. They reported that they experienced:

- Anxiety about how they should behave
- Worry about the nature of the task
- Uncertainty about what they would be expected to do
- Anxiety about the value of their contribution.

Concern about the role (which we will look at later) is very evident at this forming stage, and this means that members are focusing more on themselves as individuals than on themselves as part of a team.

As teams change this forming stage can be repeated whenever new members are recruited and inducted to the team. This process can have a detrimental effect on performance, and if it is not recognised new members may feel permanently left out and thus team coherence is lost. The forming stage could be seen as a testing time: testing oneself and, so to speak 'testing the waters'.

It is worth pointing out that some team members may see this stage as very comfortable — the polite, non-challenging behaviours and the slightly impersonal nature of interactions feel very safe. Tasks may well get tackled if this is the case, but the full benefits of team working are lost.

Storming

Tuckman and Jensen suggest that during this phase team members begin to communicate their feelings but continue to see themselves as individuals or as representatives of other teams rather than as part of the whole. This may give rise to hostility or aggression, and behaviours such as defensiveness and competitiveness can emerge. If there is a designated leader he or she may be challenged and the validity of the task may be questioned; team members may ask themselves: '*Why are we doing this?*', '*What's the point?*'. This is a very uncomfortable stage and it is possible for some would-be teams to get stuck in it. If the members have some insight into what is happening it will help them to move through it and even to see it as part of a normal, healthy process rather than as destructive. The confronting and control of conflict which seems to characterise this storming phase can, if insight can be achieved, provide valuable lessons.

Team decisions are unlikely to be reached without some degree of conflict, and learning how to work through and resolve conflict can lead to very positive outcomes if well managed. Conflict generates energy and harnessing this energy is a good way of coming to decisions. Thus the storming phase, if well facilitated, can offer a training ground for future conflict resolution.

As emotions may run high in the storming phase there is a danger that some members may opt out. They may continue as nominal team members but they will act as individuals. If this occurs, clearly team coherence is lost.

Although psychologists see these phases or stages as occurring in all groups, some teams claim that for them storming did not occur. This may be because the members were very task oriented and were not wholly aware of the team process.

Norming

This is the phase when individuals begin to see themselves as part of a whole and realise that they can work together if they accept that others have viewpoints which may be different from their own but are equally valid. The team will begin to develop essential processes and procedures to achieve the task. They begin to feel safe enough to give and receive feedback and to confront issues rather than confronting other team members. As individuals settle down they begin to co-operate and work accelerates. A side effect of this process is often the creation of in-jokes.

Performing

By the performing stage, the team has, so to speak, grown up and can work in an open and trusting way. Behaviour is characterised by openness, trust and mutual respect and support. The team works flexibly, in an atmosphere where hierarchy is of minimal importance or even irrelevant. There is little negative competitiveness, individuals are energised and sometimes even inspired.

If you were to draw a time line for your health care team, would it be possible to mark on it when it passed through these four stages and how long each took? If you think that the model does not apply as far as your team is concerned, consider why this is the case (see *Box 1*).

Think box I

On the timeline below, mark the points at which your team passed through forming, storming, norming, and performing:

$$\longrightarrow$$

If you think this model does not apply to your team, think about and write down why it did not.

If the model did not seem to 'fit' this may be because there was a very able leader, or given the fluid nature of the membership there might have been sufficient mutuality of support to outweigh any conflict at the storming stage and allow the team to move quickly to norming and performing.

Try to work through the following activity with your healthcare team (or any other team you belong to). If the model does not seem to fit, reflect why this might be (see *Box 2*).

You will have noticed that the model below has an additional phase of Mourning / Adjourning. In some cases, when the task of the team is complete, some teams may disband. When this happens there is often a sense of loss. In the context of health care this may happen when a patient is discharged and the core team for him or her will move on to another patient and perhaps another team, even though they are still under the same 'umbrella' team.

A second model of team life is represented in terms of interlocking needs which the team itself has to learn to manage. It has three elements:

- Task needs
- Individual needs
- Process needs.

These can be represented as in *Figure 2* overleaf.

The three needs affect how well a team performs, and maintaining a balance between the three is seen as crucial for success. Members can often articulate the task needs reasonably clearly (although in a storming phase they may insist that

---

Think box 2

Try to work through the following table with your healthcare team (or any other team you belong to). If the model does not seem to fit reflect why this might be:

Development stage	What does it feel like to work in a team at this stage of development?
Forming	
Storming	
Norming	
Performing	
Mourning / Adjourning	

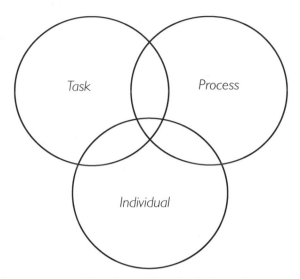

Figure 2. Interlocking team needs: task needs, individual needs, process needs.

they do not have the wherewithal to meet the needs). Perhaps we could say that the task needs are understood intellectually.

Individuals join or are delegated to teams for a variety of reasons and bring with them their own needs; if these are not realised the balance of the team can be seriously affected. Individual needs may not be so clear and may never be articulated (see *Box 3*).

Think box 3

Think about how well task needs and individual needs are met within your own team.

One healthcare team which I interviewed for this chapter felt that the task (providing home care) was paramount, and that all team effort was directed to this end. They acknowledged, however, that there was a level of discontent because many individual needs (for example, training, assistance, support) were not being met. In discussion, they agreed that as a team they had little awareness of 'process'; some members said that they did not really understand what the term means in relation to their team. In effect we could say that they were unaware of team dynamics. Process is not an easy concept and is certainly the most difficult of the three needs to grasp. We look at it in more depth later in this book, but meanwhile *Table 1* opposite may help to explore the notion of what is actually going on in a team — the process.

Table I Essential team process skills

Effective teams	Ineffective teams
Priorities — usually seek a method and criteria for solving problems at outset, rather than 'dive in'; are aware of time limitations	'Alligator' techniques — jump in with both arms and legs and jaws in motion; rarely ask: *'What's a way to solve the problem?'*, *'How should we go about it given time constraints?'*, *'What resources do we have in the team?'* *'What criteria are relevant?'*
Climate — respect for others' opinions; open to criticism and differences of opinion; little sarcasm or put-downs; atmosphere encourages thinking, discussion, reasoning and getting the job done; willingness to listen and change mindset	Either very friendly or hostile, 'jovials' do not see task seriously to avoid any conflict; 'hostiles' are full of sarcasm, put-downs which tend to make members clam up; 'bullies' force their solutions; unwillingness to change mindset
Leadership — no single pattern; elected leaders are accepted as legitimate but do not force their solutions; leadership may be shared or informal or natural leaders may guide task; time not wasted on competing for leadership, based on expertise not authority	Competition for who will lead team among two or three members; self-appointed dominant and aggressive person may take over; leader tends to force own solutions on team, does not seek involvement of potential resources
Roles — emphasis on performing task-oriented roles, but someone invariably provides for group maintenance and cohesion by good humour and wit	Absence of task or maintenance roles or domination of one is typical
Participation / Listening — circular seating arrangements chosen intuitively and facilitates balanced interaction; balanced participation utilises all team resources; good listening, few interruptions or side conversations, some functional interruption to avoid waste of time or irrelevant points; discussion is usually calmer, quieter	Many interruptions, louder conversations, sometimes shouting, often sub-groups engage in conversation, unwilling to listen to others or alter individual views
Conflict resolution — open confrontation of differences of opinion; logic and reason tend to prevail; less emotional, willingness to talk out differences, assumptions, reasons inferences and willing to change opinion based on consensus or near unanimous majority; the confrontations can involve considerable emotion	Usually more emotional and louder; much argument rather tan reasoning; tend to want to avoid conflict or difference of opinion by compromising, voting, trading-off, stubborn attachment to individual solutions; simple majority vote also used to resolve conflict

The process or 'life' of the team can be seen as separate from the other two needs, yet at the same time is integral to them. You might consider creating a similar grid for your own team to gain an insight into its process.

A third possible way of looking at a team uses the same structure as in *Figure 2* (three interlocking needs), but instead of calling one of the needs 'process' it calls it 'maintenance' (see *Figure 3*). The idea is that team members have a responsibility to engage in activities (for example reviews) which enhance the wellbeing of the team. A team needs a regular space in which to attend to team needs, to reflect on

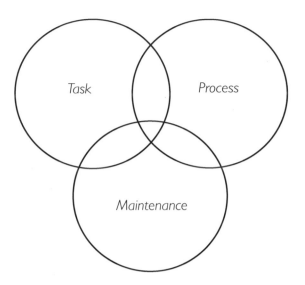

Figure 3. A third structure of team needs: task needs, process needs and maintenance needs

how as a team issues are being tackled, challenges overcome, or conflict resolved. It is the 'how' of team work which is the process. If process needs are attended to the other needs are more likely to be met and the work will be accelerated and, most importantly, the qualities essential for an effective team are more likely to result.

Review each of the models for your own team and consider which is likely to be a truer reflection of where the team is now and what might be needed to enhance it.

Tuckman BW, Jensen X (1965) Development sequence in small groups. *Psychological Bulletin* 3

CHAPTER 3

Team process

At the end of chapter 2 we looked at the characteristics of good and not so good teams. We have all been members of a group or groups of one sort or another through our lives, and this should be sound preparation for being team members. It is worth reflecting on what made your group or team 'good or 'not so good'. Try to recall a group or team of which you have been a member which left you feeling good both about yourself and about the team. Then think of a group that left you feeling bad about the team or about yourself. What made your experience of that team bad?

Think box I

Recall a group or team of which you have been a member which left you feeling good both about yourself and about the team. Then think of a group that left you feeling bad about the team or about yourself. What made your experience of that team bad?

It is very likely that the experience of a team is influenced less by what happened than by how it happened — that is, the experience was more about process than about content.

Because so much of our living and working is spent in groups or teams, a great deal of research has gone into how they function and operate. The main area of research has focused on how team members interact — that is the dynamics. The term 'dynamics' implies that the forces which interact to influence individual behaviours are not static but are fluid and are changing constantly. Even so, research seems to suggest that there are four main areas which are always in motion, and that these are the dynamics which constitute process (Boxby et al, 1986; Belbin, 1981). The four are:

1. **Communication patterns**: the verbal and non-verbal communication patterns between team members will affect the achievement or non-achievement of goals.
2. **Cohesiveness**: the team's attractiveness for its members and their

loyalty to it is significant. Highly cohesive teams have a higher positive outcome overall and more support and mutual acceptance within them.

3. **Social control:** the team has sound methods for compliance and conformity which allow it to function in an orderly way (speaking through the Chair in formal meetings is an example of social control). These rules and controls can be very helpful in managing individual behaviours so that the team task remains the focus. Time-keeping, confidentiality boundaries, attendance at meetings or events are all typical examples of a team's social control.

4. **Group Ethos:** the team will develop its own beliefs, customs and values from sharing with each other and thus create the environment within which to work. The culture or ethos should provide support, advice, willingness to test or try out strategies and a measure of universality. It should be able to develop as a learning forum, with members learning about themselves and their work through understanding of their own team process.

Think box 2

Do these four areas of dynamics underlie your health care team?
(Remember that the dynamics are fluid):

Obviously, the dynamics/process will be influenced by what type of team has come into being and indeed how it came into being. For example:

Problem-solving team: teams in this category might be committees, sub-committees or working parties (the examples are not exclusive). The team is convened to tackle problems which could not be solved by a single individual, and where team solutions offer a greater diversity of human resource and expertise, allow errors to be corrected as work proceeds, and progress increases motivation. Example:

> *A community day care centre had very limited parking facilities, which was especially difficult for some of the less mobile patients and their volunteer drivers. Frequently there were complaints that other staff were taking up spaces and pressure was particularly difficult on study days when additional visitors were present. The team was specifically tasked with overcoming the problem.*

You can perhaps see how team members might have different priorities about parking and that these would affect the dynamic within the team, which in turn would affect the eventual solution.

Think box 3

Try to find examples of problem-solving teams in your own health care setting.

Educational team (in the broadest sense of the term): which came into being to facilitate learning by team members. This type of team may be convened by one member (the individual who initiates the team's formation) or may be a collective idea. These teams are most effective if:

- There is a variety of ability
- There is a common bond (especially one of willingness to learn)
- Team teaching and/or self-managed learning are well balanced.

A group of hospice personnel felt that they needed help to work with issues of spirituality. They obtained a small grant and were able to employ the services of a consultant who ran some training sessions to help the team develop greater insight into this difficult, but crucial, area of end-of-life care.

In this case, interestingly, the team had firstly to be a problem-solving one, as they needed to obtain the grant.

Think box 4

If you have been a member of an educational team, what made the experience good (or not so good)?

Experiential team: might more properly be called 'groups' as the assumption is that the members will benefit from membership of the group itself. Therapeutic groups of course belong in this category and many healthcare providers offer therapeutic groups to their service users (substance misuse support groups are an obvious example) but the staff team and volunteers may have, for instance, an 'away day' where the purpose is to develop or maintain the team itself. This kind of activity is experiential in the sense that team members are given the opportunity and space to experience themselves as a team. Individuals are given time away from the task or problem they were formed as a team to consider and reflect on themselves as a team and on the dynamics that seem to flow within their team.

Within these three types of teams or groups research show that, whatever the context, the four areas of process seem to pertain. We can analyse each of the four in more detail.

Communication

The verbal and non-verbal communication patterns within a team will affect the achievement or non-achievement of the team goals or tasks. Non-verbal cues can give very useful data about how individuals feel about what is happening (as opposed to what might be being said or done).

It is worth looking at whether non-verbal behaviours are general rather than singular. For example, if only one member at a team meeting is sighing, yawning, doodling, then that may be to do with something personal (and possibly completely separate from the work of the team), but if the majority or even all of the members are distracted in one way or another it is team behaviour and therefore important in terms of process. If the team is reasonably mature then it should be possible to open up the issue: '*What is happening?*', '*Is everyone anxious? Tired? Bored?*', '*How can this be changed?*'. Some non-verbal behaviours may be at odds with what is actually said or contributed, and given what we know about communication (that it is 7% what we say, 38 % how we say it, and 55% non-verbal), the non-verbal communication within a team is probably a truer representation of process than the verbal communication.

Below are some cues which you might find it helpful to note in your palliative care team:

- Posture: leaning forward and showing interest; slumping in seats; sitting very stiffly; turning towards or away from other team members. Who sits next to whom at a meeting can be very indicative, as can how team members greet each other.
- Facial expressions: smiling; frowning; grimacing; casting eyes up or down; blanking out; winking (by whom to/at whom) is often very indicative.
- Gestures: pointing; nodding or shaking the head; leaning heavily on elbows; nudging the person next to them; thumbs up or down; rude gestures.
- Emotional expressions: sighs; tears; giggles; grunts; withdrawal; refusal to make eye contact.

Speech patterns

Much can be learned about team process by studying the pattern of who speaks to whom in a meeting. Have a look at the following example of a pattern of communication given in *Activity 2* and try to answer the questions.

Trying a similar experiment during a meeting of your health care team could be a useful way of determining what the communication process is, regardless of what is said by whom to whom.

Wilfred Bion, a pioneer in analysing group or team process, thought that frequency of communication between individuals was important too: the total number of contributions made by each individual team member over a specific length of time is, he thought, highly significant (Bion, 1961). If, for example, one member has made more than a third of the contributions, or if two members have contributed little or nothing, the team needs to reflect on whether this is a desirable state of affairs or whether the potential of some parts of the team is 'untapped'. If one person's contributions are significantly higher than those of others it probably signifies that those 'others' are responding rather than contributing, thus the team is not operating as a team. *Table 1* overleaf demonstrates this process.

Of course, the number of contributions does not give any indication as to how lengthy each was — the contributions may have varied from a few seconds to several minutes. A person making few contributions may have made very

Activity 2

Study the pattern of interaction below, taken over a 2 minute period. Each interaction is indicated by the arrows. Then answer the questions that follow:

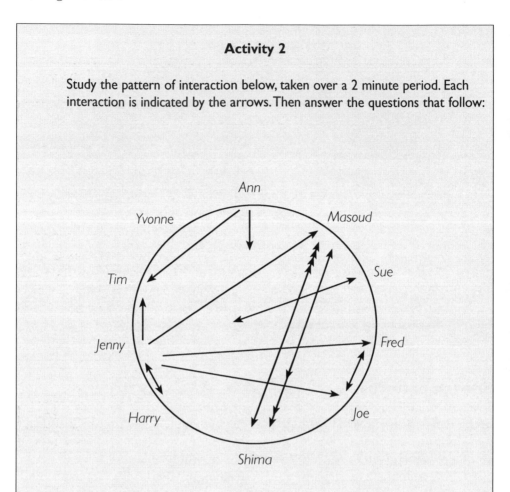

1. Who speaks to whom?

2. How many times?

3 On the basis of this record, what can you say about the pattern of participation?

4. Can you say anything about who is influential?

5. Who do you think is the group leader? What makes you think it is this person?

Source: National Extension College: Groupwork

Table 1. Example of frequency of contributions

Group member	Contributions over a 15 minute period	Total contributions
A	‖‖	5
B	‖‖‖	4
C	‖	2
D	‖‖ ‖‖	10
E	—	0
F	‖‖ ‖‖ ‖‖	13

lengthy comments, similarly someone making very frequent interventions may make only brief comments, therefore a further method, which indicates time, can be made by recording who was speaking and for how long over a specific period of time. It is then possible to observe who was contributing at length and who made short or frequent contributions (see *Table 2*).

Table 2. Communications sampled at 5 minute intervals

5 minute intervals	5	10	15	20	25	30	35	40	45	50	55	60
Member speaking	D	A	F	F	F	F	B	F	D	A	A	F

Think box 6

What can you learn from the record in *Table 2?*

We can see from this sample table that team member F seemed to dominate the meeting, while members C and E made no contribution at all. This type of recording can be useful, but of course it tends to apply only to meetings. It may be difficult, if not impossible, for a team member to record in this way because in meetings we are usually too busy interacting and 'getting on with the job' to be able to stand back and reflect on process. If possible, a team meeting can be audio or visually recorded (mature teams should not find this objectionable) and an analysis attempted in order to answer the question: *'What is happening in our team?'*. This need not feel threatening as the aim is not to find fault with the team but to explore its process. Consider the following example:

A practice team had their weekly case discussion meeting recorded on video. Members were at first rather self-conscious, but soon became absorbed in the task and forgot the camera. At their next 'away day' some formal input was given about team process and the film was used to demonstrate their own process. Afterwards, team members agreed that they had much greater insight and felt very strongly that practice would be enhanced.

Think box 7

How amenable would your health care team be to exploring in this way?

It has also been suggested that the sequence of interaction between members is a significant indicator of team process. *Table 3* is an example of how the flow of interactions between team members might be recorded:

Table 3. Contributions to group members

	A	B	C	D	All	Total	%
A	—	4	2	6	2	14	28
B	1	—	1	3	5	10	20
C	2	0	—	5	0	7	14
D	6	4	5	—	4	19	38
Total	9	8	8	14	11	50 / 50	100
% total	18	16	16	28	22	100	

If we took team member D as an example we can see that she or he made nineteen (19) contributions to the overall interactions, taking up about 38% of the time. Team member D was addressed by others in the team 14 times. Team member D is therefore seen as having an important role in the proceedings. Although this method of recording is most obviously for times when the team members are all together in one place, it is also possible to note this kind of frequency in a team when it is not static — perhaps over the course of one week. Consider the scenario below:

The ward manager had picked up in supervision several comments from team members which amounted to a sense that they felt overwhelmed by one member. This member was the newest recruit to the service and it was acknowledged that he had much to contribute, but that there was nevertheless some sense of discomfort. As one team member put it: 'It's as if he sort of wants to have his say all the time and although some of us do make an effort, it's not easy and some of us don't bother any more, we just listen. Don't get me wrong, what he says often is very good, but others have good ideas too.'

The manager was concerned not to disrupt the good team ethos which had built up over several years; she was equally anxious not to offend the new member or to dampen his enthusiasm and so waste his expertise. She kept a flow diagram (like the one in Activity 2) over a week and noted the contributions to and from the team members as they came and went. She was able to offer this to the new member, who realised how his interactions might be seen. The manager followed this up with a further week's recording and noted that the frequency was more evenly balanced across the team.

There is one further technique of recording communication patterns. This technique records the sequence rather than the flow and enables us to draw conclusions similar to those we have looked at. We can record in a simple linear way the person(s) making each contribution in sequence. It is then possible to follow the pattern of communication over a given length of time (see *Table 4*):

Table 4. Pattern of communication in a 2 minute sequence

D	A	D	A	D	B	D	B	A	D	A	D

In the case of *Table 4* we can see that team members D and A dominated in the time span of the recording. There were two contributions from B and none at all from C, who not only remained silent but was also not addressed by the others. It is possible from this method of recording to establish not only how many contributions each person made, but whether these were scattered throughout the time frame, or all at the beginning or end. In the example, D began and ended the interaction. With this method it is possible to monitor whether there are sub-groups developing within a team, as well as who might be dominating or not contributing. The team can then begin to take steps to look at whether and how it wants to change.

Cohesiveness

The second feature of the four aspects of team dynamics is cohesiveness. Team process is affected by how attractive membership is to individuals. Loyalty is an important component of cohesiveness and can be measured by indicators such as attendance (sickness rates are often a good indicator), willingness to accept the norms of the team — for example in relation to confidentiality. If you remind yourself of the Tuckman model of the life of a team, you will recall that in the forming or storming phases individuals may be asking: '*Why are we here?*', '*What are we doing or supposed to be doing?*'. In the norming phase, as the team begins to find its feet, certain norms emerge. If people are persistently late, or if they find reasons (excuses) for absenteeism or even drop out altogether, what might this indicate about the attractiveness of membership? Research seems to show that many people continue as nominal members of their team but are not wholly involved, in effect they have dropped out or are doing their own thing, even though they may still be nominally team members. This can have a powerfully detrimental effect on cohesiveness.

In a diverse healthcare team, boundaries (for example of confidentiality) may not always be clear. Counsellors, social workers, nurses, doctors, complementary therapists, volunteers may all see themselves as adhering to their own profession's codes of conduct. If a team can develop its own norms about important issues its cohesiveness will be enhanced. Consider the scenario below:

A community home care team, where many patients and their relatives were 'shared' and therefore known to many team members, agreed to name their patients only as A, B, C, etc., unless all the team were together. This was especially important in a rural community where families and their histories were known and where any leakage of information could have had social consequences.

Highly cohesive teams are researched as having a higher outcome overall. They also have the bonus of being more supportive to each other.

Think Box 8

On a scale of 1 to 10, how cohesive would you say your team is? If the score is low, what do you think is needed to enhance cohesiveness?

Social control

It may seem rather restrictive to consider that an effective team might need social control, but if it is to achieve its goals, targets, tasks (ie if the content is to have a positive outcome), it will need to function in a reasonably ordered way. This is especially important in palliative care where the therapeutic input spans such a wide spectrum. Consider the scenario below:

A member of a palliative support service called to offer a family help with obtaining benefits and was met with a very cold response by the patient's mother. Eventually it transpired that hers was the fourth visit that day, that the mother had missed going out to shop and that the patient (her 14-year-old daughter) had had to be disturbed twice, as a result. Eventually the mother apologised and acknowledged that: 'We need all the help you can give us, but I just wish it was a bit more organised'.

The ways in which a team applies methods for gaining compliance, agreement or conformity is the process of 'social control'. In a previous example I mentioned speaking through the Chair at meetings. We may realise that this is not always obeyed except in very formal meetings – but the process is nevertheless in place; the team has accepted that some form of order is necessary for smooth functioning. This does not mean that the controls should be restrictive or curb individual initiatives, but that they are a necessary aspect of the dynamic.

Good methods of social control develop confidence between team members, and thus contribute to cohesiveness. For example, in a diverse healthcare team it is important to know where members are at any one time should they be needed. A system is needed to ensure this is essential, otherwise patient care is in danger of becoming haphazard rather than well structured. Good social control facilitates the development of:

- Trust
- Improved flow of communication
- Joint problem-solving
- Joint decision-making
- Ways of communicating with other teams.

These positive dynamics will have a powerful effect on patient care.

Activity 3

Try to list the social controls which exist in your health care team.

Norms of behaviour and clear understanding about boundaries and about acceptable/unacceptable conduct will help to achieve the aims and tasks confronting the team, thus process enhances content.

Think box 9

To what extent do you think the social controls you listed in Activity 3 affect team effectiveness and hence enhance patient care?

Team ethos

The fourth element of process is probably the most important. A good team will develop its own culture and this will include the beliefs, customs and values shared by team members. The ethos which develops will have a profound effect upon the emotional and psychological environment in which the team operates. The culture should be supportive and respectful and should offer many learning (in the broadest sense of the word) opportunities. There should be some sense of universality. As one member of a health care team put it:

> *'We all know where we're going. We may not always agree about how we'll get there, but we believe in the destination'.*

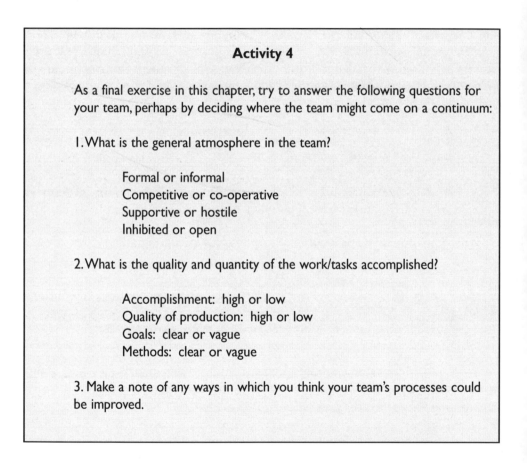

Activity 4

As a final exercise in this chapter, try to answer the following questions for your team, perhaps by deciding where the team might come on a continuum:

1. What is the general atmosphere in the team?

    Formal or informal
    Competitive or co-operative
    Supportive or hostile
    Inhibited or open

2. What is the quality and quantity of the work/tasks accomplished?

    Accomplishment: high or low
    Quality of production: high or low
    Goals: clear or vague
    Methods: clear or vague

3. Make a note of any ways in which you think your team's processes could be improved.

Bales, R.F. (1950) *Interactive Process Analysis*. Addison Wesley, Massachussets

Bion, W.R. (1961) *Experiences in Groups and other Papers*. Basic Books, New York

Boxby P, Lawton R, Hastings C (1986) *The Superteam Solution*. Basic Books, New York

CHAPTER 4

The individual within the team

'When a team outgrows individual performance and learns <u>team</u> confidence, excellence becomes a reality.'

This quotation (Felz and Liogg, 1988) exemplifies what we mentioned earlier: an important aspect of team work is that the whole (the team) is greater than the sum of its parts (the individuals who make up the team). The diversity of experience and perspectives of team members generates deeper thinking about tasks and better analysis of them. This can also lead to greater team (as opposed to self) awareness whereby the team grows in consciousness of its own effectiveness and will begin to talk about process (as opposed to content). The diversity of individuals means that within the team members will take on specific roles and this will contribute to the overall dynamic.

There have been many attempts to categorise the roles adopted within teams and the behaviours attendant upon the roles which individuals choose to adopt. In this chapter we look at some of the models which have attempted to define team roles and behaviours. Understanding how people act within a team is critical if the tasks and targets are to be achieved to their optimum level.

Team roles

Belbin (1981) suggests that there are nine roles which team members might adopt. As you look at each, try to identify whether the model is applicable to individuals within your health care team. The roles are:

- Shaper
- Team worker
- Resource investigator
- Monitor / evaluator
- 'Plant'
- Completer / finisher
- Implementer
- Co-ordinator
- Specialist

Some of the labels are self explanatory, but it is worth considering some of the behaviours associated with each because each role can have a negative or positive effect on team performance.

Shapers

These are members who tend to want to organise (shape) the team in the way they think it can best achieve the task. If a team seems stuck (perhaps in the norming stage) a shaper can be very useful in getting things moving. On the other hand, some members may see him or her as bossy and over-directive and this can have a negative effect on team process, even though it may accelerate the content. As one member of a care team interviewed for this chapter rather amusingly put it: *'It's as if she's sort of telling us to pull our socks up, when we're quite happy to have them rumpled around our ankles'*. An over-strong shaper can upset the balance within a team but can be invaluable if there are deadlines to be met. There can also be conflict if the team contains more than one shaper. Consider the scenario below:

> *'A practice-based care service learned that a substantial grant for providing home care support was likely to become available, but the application process was competitive and very complex, and involved considerable form-filling. A team was created and tasked with getting the application filled in a short space of time, and with making it as convincing as possible. There was considerable diversity of opinion among team members as to what the various components of home care might be and the relative importance of each. Deadline day was approaching and the application forms were no nearer completion. Eventually one member of the team took charge and focused the team solely on the task. The application was successful, but some individuals on the team did not feel that it fully represented a consensus, even though they were pleased at their success in obtaining a grant.'*

In this scenario we can see the value of a shaper in terms of task, but also note that process may have suffered. Balancing the two can be difficult and a mature team will be able to maintain a good balance.

Resource investigator

This person will not only be a person who conducts much of the practical research which the group might need (in the example above, this was the person who had actually found out about the grant and obtained the forms), but also will ensure that all the resources within the team are being met. A fully effective team will utilise all the expertise contained within it, but frequently this does not happen. There may be many reasons, for example members are too shy to voice their opinions, some may not wish to seem boastful if they say they can do certain things, some may hope that by not sharing anything about their views or talents they will not be called on to contribute, etc. The resource investigator will be alert to the dynamics and try to ensure that the full capability of the individuals is known.

Think box 1

How fully to you think the capabilities of individuals in your own team are being utilised?

Plant

This is an interesting team role. The plant can have unfortunate connotations as a term since it has acquired association with spying and covert policing! However that is not its meaning as far as team membership is concerned. (Even so, in dysfunctional teams there can be a tendency to scapegoat someone as a management 'plant' in the negative sense of the word.) A team member who adopts the role of plant is more likely to be a person who is able to see things from an outside perspective or, as the modern idiom has it, 'can think outside the box'. Sometimes they will take a 'devil's advocate' position in order to ensure that the team considers more than one aspect of its work. The role was expressed to me in this way:

'I see myself as a sort of prism. The team can get caught up in tunnel vision sometimes, or in seeing things only as either/or, when it may well be possible to do both. What I try to do is throw a bit of light onto other perspectives. I think sometimes the others find me a bit of a nuisance, but if we are to look at all the possibilities, someone has to show that there's more than one way up the mountain (if that isn't mixing my metaphors too much!).'

Activity 1

Work through the other roles, keeping your own team in mind.

      Team worker
      Monitor / evaluator
      Completer / finisher
      Implementer
      Co-ordinator
      Specialist

The team wheel

This interesting model was developed by two researchers (Margerison and McCann, 1988) who consider that nine essential team activities can be distinguished and that a preference for how a member works will result in what role she or he will adopt within the team. The nine essential team activities are:

- **Advising**: gathering information and reporting it to the team (this may remind you of the role of resource investigator)
- **Innovating**: creating ideas and experimenting with them
- **Promoting**: finding opportunities and presenting them for consideration
- **Developing**: assessing and testing the feasibility of any new approaches or ideas
- **Organising**: establishing and implementing in order to 'make things work'
- **Producing**: concluding and delivering whatever the team 'product' may be
- **Inspecting**: checking that the 'product' actually works as the team intended
- **Maintaining**: upholding and safeguarding standards and processes
- **Linking**: co-ordinating and integrating the work of others.

Think box 2

Take a moment to reflect on whether these are the activities which your healthcare team engages in, or needs to engage in. Are there any significant gaps?

The model then moves on to measure how preferences for a way of working in a team can be measured in four main ways. The preference has a powerful impact on both team work and individual performance and satisfaction within the team. These four preferences are:

1. Preference for introverted or extraverted work
2. Preference for balancing creative work with practical work
3. Preference for analysing decisions and a belief in their importance and validity
4. Preference for working in a flexible way or in a structured way.

Margerison and McCann (1988) claim that combining these preferences within a team has a powerful influence on motivation, job satisfaction, team work, learning and development. From these preferences they conclude that there are eight roles which people adopt in teams, and they illustrate this in *Figure 1*.

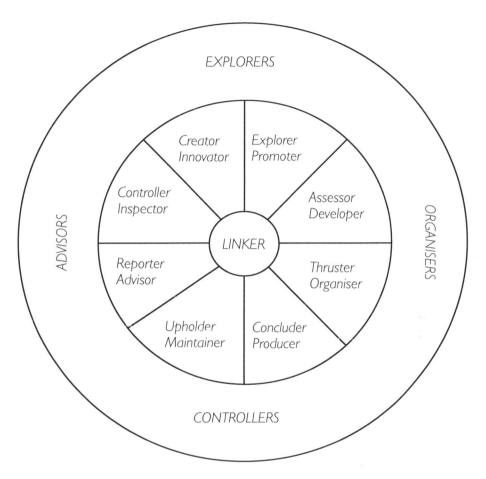

Figure 1. The sections of the team wheel. Source: Margerison and McCann (1988)

Reporter / Advisor
This team member is a supporter or helper in terms of team work. He or she collects information, dislikes being rushed and is likely to be knowledgeable and flexible.

Creator / Innovator
This person is likely to be imaginative and focused on the future, he or she is creative, often enjoys complexity of tasks, and usually likes researching.

Explorer / Promoter
As you might expect the explorer is good at persuading others and can be very good at selling ideas. Promoters are usually outgoing and good at work which is stimulating or exciting but can get bored easily.

Assessor / Developer

Predictably, this is the team member who is an experimenter and who will use analytical abilities to weigh up ideas and is often very good at project type work.

Thruster / Organiser

This is the 'shaper' of the earlier model. He or she is very focused on the task and on getting results and will often set up systems and networks in order to achieve them. He or she is likely to be the team's decision maker.

Concluder / Producer

This useful role is likely to be from a very practical person who likes schedules and plans to ensure that pride can be taken in the 'product'. He or she values efficiency and can be impatient if the team appears to lack it.

Controller / Inspector

As the name of the role implies, an inspector would be strong on detail and will examine the 'product' for flaws and is keen on standards and procedures.

Upholder / Maintainer

This is the team's loyal supporter, with a strong sense of right and wrong both in terms of the team and in terms of the team's 'product'. He or she is strongly motivated by values and by what the team's purpose is, and can sometimes seem over cautious.

The '**linker**' role is shared by all members of the team.

The roles and work preferences in this model clearly reflect the psychology of the emotions and desires which are brought to team work. If there is poor alignment or a mismatch then the dynamics are bound to be affected. This indicates how important team selection is, and whilst it is important for individuals to contribute what they feel most comfortable with, it is the responsibility of the team to make sure that all tasks are covered.

An advantage might be that people tend to work better if they are able to work with what they prefer. A disadvantage might be that the dynamics of a

---

Think box 3

What do you see as the advantages and disadvantages of the model, in terms of your own team?

---

group are, by their nature, not fixed and this could lead to conflict as people develop within the team or as membership changes.

People are guided by four basic emotional needs or drives. These are:

- **Acquire:** not only things/objects, but less tangible objects such as social status
- **Bond**: form connections with other individuals and be part of a group
- **Comprehend**: to understand what we are doing and why we are doing it
- **Defend**: protect against external threats and promote justice.

Think box 4

Some researchers contend that these four drives underlie everything that we do. Do you agree or disagree?

Whether you think that there may be more or different drives, you can perhaps agree that to satisfy the emotional need/drive to bond can best be satisfied by a culture which promotes team work, collaboration, openness and friendship. The other drives may not be so dependent upon team membership, but team dynamics suggest that they are important. For instance, the drive to comprehend is best met by working on tasks that are meaningful, interesting and challenging. Fair, trustworthy and transparent processes help people to meet their drive to defend.

Think box 5

If you look round your own healthcare team, are you able to confirm that these findings are valid? Is there any way in which your team could be enhanced by awareness of the findings?

Bales (1950) described a range of behaviours which he claimed can be observed as exhibited by members of any group/team, in almost any situation. He invented a system called *Interactive Process Analysis* to measure team dynamics. He suggested that members' behaviours (both verbal and non-verbal) can be described under two main headings: 'task orientation', and 'socio-emotional orientation'.

Members of the task type are mostly concerned with getting the job (whatever they perceive it to be) done and in order to do so they engage in a variety of behaviours which are intended to clarify what the task is and to move towards a conclusion. This will mean that they:

- Ask questions
- Give opinions, suggestions, information which they see as relevant to the task
- Ask for direction, suggestions and information
- Tend to repeat and clarify what others have said.

Think box 6

You will notice that Bales (1950) indicates that socio-emotional members actually show these positive attributes, they do not just feel them. What would you say these positives contribute to an effective team?

Some of your suggestions might include:
> They foster cohesion (the team sees itself as a team) and a sense of solidarity
> They lessen tension if any humour used is appropriate
> The culture of the team takes into account the feelings of members, as well as the more logical, practical aspects of the task.

A good team is likely to have a balance of task orientated and socio-emotional roles because the two complement each other. How well balanced in this respect do you see your healthcare team?

Task orientated team members are not always concerned about the *feelings* of other members; this is not because they are uncaring, but because their first priority is to get the job done. Consider the scenario below:

'A bereavement support group was asked to compile a database of agencies who had been helpful to them in their loss. The group thought that this would be a positive thing to come out of their grief, but quite serious conflict arose between those who wanted to research and collate information and those who still saw the primary reason for their meetings was to help with grief. The task orientated members thought that they could move back to their original purpose once the database was completed. It took very skilled leadership to balance the dynamic.'

If you look back at the earlier models, you may see that the roles we described there can be clearly observed in task orientated members.

Bales (1950) observed that members of the socio-emotional type were either positive or negative in their contribution to the team's dynamic. The positives include:

- Showing satisfaction and giving help
- Making jokes, using humour
- Showing understanding, acceptance, agreement
- Showing solidarity.

On the other hand, some socio-emotional roles are negative, which may create problems in a team's dynamic. Negative aspects include:

- Disagreeing (often just for the sake of it)
- Refusing to be helpful and putting others down
- Showing a degree of antagonism or even rejection of other members
- 'Opting out' by becoming withdrawn.

Think box 7

Within your team, who has the responsibility for dealing with problematic issues caused by role conflict? Are there any ways in which these negatives could have a positive effect on a team's dynamic?

Most of us can think of or have been members of teams where these aspects have been evident, and it is worth reflecting on how they might be resolved and by whom.

One positive which can result, especially if there is **group** challenge of the negatives, is that there can be a growth in self-awareness and hence of learning in its broadest sense. Consider the scenario below:

'A volunteer worker for an end-of-life service could not understand why she was never asked to be a member of one of the development teams which the service was creating. She became quite bitter about this because she felt she had a great deal to contribute and was full of ideas. She also felt that her loyalty to the service deserved recognition and reward. Unfortunately, as a member of the original team which had set up the service, she had gained a reputation for always contradicting others and tending to indicate that their ideas for the service had no value and should be rejected in favour of hers. Sometimes her ideas were, indeed, better.

Eventually the director of the project, who was not a member of the team, had the unpleasant task of asking the volunteer to leave the team as other members were threatening a mass resignation if she did not go.'

A mature team could have dealt with the scenario above in a rather different way which might have actually helped the volunteer's self-awareness, but the case above illustrates how powerfully negative roles can affect a team's dynamic and can sometimes mean that the task itself is never accomplished.

Think box 8

Consider how your healthcare team might have resolved the problem in the scenario above.

Activity 2

As a team member yourself — either presently or in the future — it is worthwhile considering which of the roles we have looked at you see yourself as 'fitting in'. Individuals may fit more than one role, or be a mixture of several roles; this is because the very nature of a team's dynamic is that it is not static and roles may change or be affected by the changing dynamic.

When you have thought about the role you mostly adopt in your healthcare team try to answer the following questions to enlarge your awareness of how you and others behave in your team.

Ask yourself the following questions:

1. Who do I find difficult?
2. What behaviour do I find hardest to handle?
3. What effect does this person/these people have on me?
4. How do I respond?
5. How is this member/these members affecting:
      the group
      the task
6. What might be the reason for this behaviour?
7. In what ways might the group be influencing this behaviour?

Bales RF (1950) *Interactive Process Analysis.* Addison Wesley, Massachusetts

Belbin RM (2003) *Management Teams: Why they succeed or fail.* Butterworth Heinemann, London

Belbin RM (1993) *Team Roles at Work.* Butterworth Heinemann, London

Bion WR (1961) *Experiences in Groups and other Papers.* Basic Books, New York

Margerison CJ, McCann DJ (1988) *Team Management Profiles.* Basic Books, New York

CHAPTER 5

Roles and role behaviour

Team roles could perhaps be categorised as:

- Task roles
- Team maintenance roles
- Task and maintenance roles
- Non-functional roles.

Task roles

Task roles would seem to be those functions which are required for selecting and carrying out the team task or, in process terms, the content. Are you able to identify the following roles within your healthcare team?

- *Initiating activity*: proposing solutions, suggesting new ideas, re-defining the problem, beginning a new or different attack on the problem or a new way of organising existing material
- *Seeking information*: asking for clarification, requesting additional information or facts
- *Seeking opinions*: looking for other members' expressions of feelings about the task, trying to gain clarification about values, and about suggestions and ideas
- *Giving information*: relating own experiences to illustrate points about the task, or offering facts and generalisations
- *Giving opinions*: stating a belief about a suggestion, particularly if the idea is new, trying to re-define issues and problems, reorganising any existing material
- *Elaborating*: trying to envisage how proposals might work out if they were to be tried, trying to 'make sense' of possible outcomes
- *Co-ordinating*: demonstrating any relationships between various ideas and suggestions, 'pulling it all together'
- *Summarising*: trying to re-state where the team is at at various stages and trying to encapsulate the final team position.

Read the following transcript of a meeting of a bereavement

support team (recorded and used with their permission). The team visit the bereaved in their own homes and call themselves the BVs (bereavement visitors). The team is quite mature and although the membership changes, there is a core membership which has remained unchanged. Meetings of the full team are infrequent, although members have many *ad hoc* points of contact — they telephone each other and meet in twos or threes if they think it helps their work or if they feel in need of support. All members are volunteers; some members have professional expertise in bereavement work but contribute voluntarily to this service. The meeting transcribed below has been called to consider setting up a telephone contact service. Until now, all support work has been face-to-face, but there has been a feeling that too much valuable time is spent travelling and that more bereaved people could be helped by telephone or even by electronic means. As you read, jot down any examples of members fulfilling the task roles listed. At the point where this transcript starts the meeting has been going on for some time. Three members, who were fairly new to the team, had said that they did not have sufficient experience to form an opinion. They said that they would prefer to listen to the views of the more experienced BVs before coming to any sort of conclusion:

A *'I think we should give it a try. The numbers keep on growing, which I suppose shows that we're doing a good job, but there just aren't enough of us to go round. It doesn't mean we'd have to give up what we do now, just do something different as well.'*

B *'I don't know...I'd just like to see how it would actually work. Is there anything we could look at to see exactly what we're supposed to do? I mean, do we know of any other group that uses telephone contact? I just don't feel I know enough about it.'*

C *'I think that's a good point, but what I'd really like to know is how we all feel about changing in this way. I've been doing this work since it was started and for me the whole point is actually being with someone. Somehow it seems to go against the grain to be remote on the phone. I may be a bit old fashioned, but I wonder how our clients would feel talking to a telephone or a computer (supposing they have one — has any one checked?). It goes against everything I believe in about bereavement care.'*

D *'I don't know if it helps, but I have done some work with the Samaritans, and they seem to be successful with phone contact. And there's a lot of interest in on-screen counselling, according to the people on my counselling course.'*

A *'I think we're going round and round and getting nowhere. We should really be thinking about whether or not we want to give it a try and see how it goes.*

What do they call it in business — a pilot scheme? We could keep a careful record of how it goes and then decide whether to go for it permanently. What do you think?'

E   *'If we did that how would it work? What phone number or numbers could we use — I don't suppose we'd all want to be rung up any old time. Would someone have to be sort of on-duty? If so, how would that work? Would we have to take turns in organising the rota? I don't have a computer, so I wouldn't be able to make that kind of contact, but I'd like to know how it works.'*

D   *'I'm not sure where we've got to, but it seems as if two things are coming out — that we ought at least to give it a try and that would mean working out the logistics of the thing, or that it's not the way we want to run the support because we don't believe it's what we or the bereaved want. Is that a fair summing up?'*

A   *'Yes, fair enough. I'm all for a trial run, but it will be difficult and I'm prepared to go along with what we all want.'*

What can you deduce about this team's process?

Team maintenance roles

Team maintenance roles are the functions needed for strengthening and maintaining team life and activities. They include:

- *Expressing*: (by verbalising) what the team's feelings seem to be, being sensitive to what the emotional climate seems to be, sensing unspoken conflicts and distress
- *Standard setting*: ensuring that the team keeps to its values (which may have been formally agreed) when the team chooses its work or focus, especially as far as decision making is concerned
- *Being a 'gate-keeper'*: keeping the team on task, by ensuring that all members contribute and thus ensuring that the team is working as a team
- *Encouraging*: being warm and friendly, being responsive to others, valuing and praising the contributions of others, being accepting of differences.

The transcript below is what a new member of a community team said about the team maintenance role:

'When I first came to St—'s I was very nervous. This was my first job in community care and I had moved from a rather dysfunctional oncology team in the hospital — don't get me wrong — it wasn't anyone's fault, it was just that there were too many institutional changes and too few people had good training. We all seemed to be "doing our own thing", if you see what I mean and there wasn't really any team spirit. So you can see why I was nervous — I kept asking myself whether I'd be accepted and whether I'd actually be a good team player...Anyway it's been a wonderful eye opener. Two of the team in particular have really helped me to see what teamwork is all about. They were meticulous about including me in all case discussions (even though I thought I should shut up for a while!) and asked me to compare ways of working between hospital and community care. I really liked the way they keep relating what we're doing to the principles of care. One of them picked up that one or two members seemed unhappy and got them to talk about it. What's interesting looking back on these first six months is that neither of these people was the designated team leader, who seemed quite content to take a back seat! I didn't notice this at the time — I've only just realised it!'

Think box I

How important do you think team maintenance functions are? Is it the responsibility of a team leader to fulfil this role?

Task and maintenance functions

Task and maintenance functions are crucially important for a team's health and effectiveness. A team member fulfilling both functions is invaluable and is likely to be very process orientated, as the role will require a range of contributions:

- *Relieving tensions*: often by the use of humour or by changing the context of a task
- *Mediating*: sometimes the energy in a team which the diversity of membership generates can spill over into acrimony and dissent, rather than creativity. The function of mediating facilitates compromise and creates conciliation of the differences
- *Diagnosing*: this may come about as a result of mediating. There will be an attempt to determine the sources of difficulty and to find appropriate ways of resolving them. This may involve analysing blocks to progress and this is a good example of where the task and maintenance roles overlap

- *Testing out for team consensus*: even if the member is not a designated leader, he or she will often attempt what would be called in book-keeping a trial balance — that is, there might be a sort of testing as to whether the team was ready to come to some sort of whole decision; this has sometimes been called 'sending up trial balloons', the idea being that if a possible decision (the balloon) is floated, it may be possible to gauge whether the team is ready to commit to it.
- *Evaluating*: this may have a more process than maintenance aspect, as the function is to measure progress or success with the task against the team's standards or norms.

Ideally, in a fully functioning team all members will adopt both task and maintenance roles at any one time. In this way the dynamic, although it is never static, will be positive and creative.

Think box 2

If you have been or are a member of a productive team would you agree that its effectiveness has resulted from a combination of task and maintenance roles by members? Or perhaps you can recall a dysfunctional team where the combination did not exist.

Non-functional roles

Non-functional roles tend to be negative and do not contribute to the dynamics of cohesion, social control, or ethos. Some examples might be:

- *Blocking*: deliberately interfering with progress by raising irrelevant issues or those which have only a very limited association with what the team task is. Ideas are often rejected without serious consideration. This can irritate others, especially those who are very task-focused, and so this can be detrimental to process
- *Overly aggressive*: trying to enhance own status by criticising or devaluing others and/or their ideas; sometimes there is impatience or even hostility, under the guise of '*we just ought to get on with the job*' or '*I'm only being honest*'
- *Overly personal*: sometimes personal experience can be a useful contribution, but the non-functional aspect arises when personal history is not relevant to the task and when it is expressing non-team points

of view. A real danger to the dynamic here is that the whole group can become anecdotal in meetings and lose focus so that it becomes a collection of individuals rather than a team

- *Competitive*: a tendency (especially if a team has a designated leader) to vie with other team members to produce the best ideas in order to impress (especially to impress the leader), rather to foster team spirit or ethos
- *Sympathy seeking*: people join, or are put in, teams for a variety of reasons, and this can be a strength but can sometimes upset the dynamic if the team is being used to solve personal problems or misfortunes. The role is often characterised by a member who is self-disparaging — that is, they put themselves rather than other people down. The result can be that the team begins to focus its energies on helping one person, rather than on operating as a team
- *Special pleading*: this is not unlike sympathy seeking, but this non-functional role involves the member trying to manipulate the group by subverting the task to his or her own agenda
- *Clowning*: the team dynamic is lost because the members are distracted by habitual joking or amusing disruption
- *Self-seeking*: talking over others, drawing attention to self by a variety of behaviours such as yawning, sighing, fidgeting or offering ludicrous suggestions solely to gain attention.

These non-functional roles have sometimes been linked to immaturity because they seem to resemble the sort of attention seeking of a somewhat spoiled child or a disgruntled adolescent. A mature team should have only minimal examples of non-functional roles, partly because the dynamic would have outgrown them in Tuckman's storming phase (see *Activity 1*).

Behaviours of individuals (especially those acting out non-functional roles), and sometimes the collective behaviour of a team, can be counterproductive to its purpose. In the scenario of *Activity 1* opposite, the mass resignation meant that the possibility of a bedded hospice was considerably delayed.

Observers of problem solving teams suggest that they can often identify behaviours which are contrary to those which will achieve the allotted task, even when the task is self imposed. Bion (1961) whose pioneering work we mentioned earlier, suggested that this was because of three basic states which he claimed all groups and teams move through as part of the team dynamic. These are:

- Fight < > flight
- Dependency
- Pairing

- *Fight*: fighting in a team can take a variety of forms. The team may find

---

Activity I

The following scenario demonstrates how destructive of ethos it can be when a team contains too many non-functional roles. As you read, try to think how a mature team, or your own healthcare team might have resolved this dilemma:

'A hospice-at-home had grown from very modest beginnings to a large organisation serving both a city and its surrounding areas. As the senior nurse manager put it: "If you'd told me when we had those first coffee mornings and jumble sales what we'd grow to, I'd never have believed it". The organisation has a board of governors who advise on policy and on broader issues of finance, but who have very little to do with the day-to-day running of the palliative care provision. For some time, there has been the possibility that the organisation might aspire to a purpose built establishment, allowing for in-patient care and the expansion of the complementary activities which are seen as therapeutic. A team was formed to investigate this possibility. Their task involved matters of finance, accommodation, additional/alternative staffing and a range of other issues. The team leader (a governor) had very strong views as to how the possibility could become reality and seemed intent on driving through her own vision, which was sound enough but took little account of the practitioners' vision. Partly in an attempt to counteract this, a representative for the relatives (her husband had died in the care of the organisation) repeatedly described how good it had been for her husband to die at home and that a bedded hospice was not a good thing. As the new initiative, should it ever materialise, would offer new posts, a particularly ambitious team member was keen to impress with his ideas and tended to dismiss those of others except for those of the team leader. When discussion got heated one of the volunteers tried to help by telling jokes about the early days of the organisation, which clearly irritated some who tended to ignore or "switch off" when this happened. After several meetings it became evident that the task was getting lost in the negative dynamic. Several members resigned and eventually a new team had to be formed.'

---

itself witnessing an almost gladiatorial combat between two or more members and the fight may have nothing to do with the battle of ideas (the content) going on at the surface of the team. The fight is to do with process and is often about 'politics' or values. It can exist in healthcare teams where values of team members and how they should be effected may vary considerably. This can be a serious bone of contention but is rarely overtly stated, and the 'fight' gets shifted to something else which the team is working on or with, which it may have nothing to do with in fact. Thus a fairly easily resolvable disagreement about something can become the battlefield for a hidden dispute. Alternatively, a sub-group or one person may make a bid to take over the leadership of the team. If the team is generally unhappy they may support the bid for power but this can be risky, as their (possibly unconscious) effort may seriously disrupt the team's dynamic for the sake of one person. Being dissatisfied with the leader can almost become a game and a way of avoiding addressing the team task and may be part of forming or of storming.

- *Flight*: Since a team, particularly in its forming stage, may for various reasons be reluctant to see itself as a team, all sorts of avoiding behaviours may occur, for example complaints about the room or chat about the weather. One of the biggest dangers to team cohesiveness is prolonged silence — individuals take flight into not contributing and if this continues for too long the dynamic may not recover. With this type of 'flight' members are physically present but not present intellectually or emotionally. In more extreme examples, some individuals may take flight more literally and actually drop out.

- *Dependency*: some teams may try to get all their work done through one person which makes nonsense of the team as a resource. Individuals may feel that their contribution is in some way not valued, or not valuable, or feel that one person is so knowledgeable or charismatic that everything can be left to him or her. If the whole team becomes dependent in this way it becomes a sort of scapegoating of the person chosen to do the work. .

- *Pairing*: sometimes two members of a team will form a sort of sub-set and carry on a dialogue — often in whispers or asides — not geared to the task or to the needs of the team. The sense of exclusion felt by other members and often by the team leader, if there is one, can be both hurtful and disruptive to process. Divisive pairing can also allow the team to imagine that the pair are somehow superior and that they will eventually sort out any problems, so there is no need for anyone else to contribute and of course this then becomes a form of 'flight'. Bion (1961) thought that all teams and groups moved in and out of these states and that being aware of them can help to strengthen teams and enable them to tolerate ambiguity and ambivalence. By this he meant that by moving in and out of these states, the members of a mature (in the sense of 'grown up') team are able to accept and hold conflicting feelings towards an individual or institution, and avoid splitting them into good or bad. The team is then effective and productive.

Think box 3

How much evidence do you have that these states are present in any team that you belong to?

Activity 2

If you can remind yourself of the ways in which team communication can be analysed, as a last exercise in this chapter work out what is going on in the following examples.

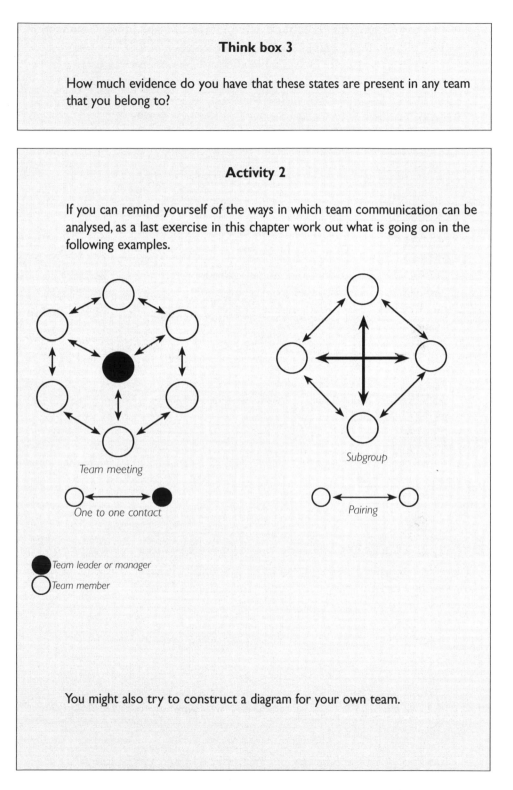

Team meeting

One to one contact

Subgroup

Pairing

Team leader or manager

Team member

You might also try to construct a diagram for your own team.

Bion WR (1961) *Experiences in Groups and other Papers.* Basic Books, New York

Klein J (1961) *Working with Groups.* Hutchinson, Boston

CHAPTER 6

Team leaders and leadership

Occasionally teams are unstructured in the sense that they do not have a designated leader. Unstructured groups were originally (and still are) used for therapeutic reasons or for personal development where the very activity of belonging to a group is reckoned to be helpful to its distressed members or to those wishing to increase their self awareness. The success of group therapy has meant that unstructured groups have been found to be helpful outside the clinical setting and they are now set up to offer support in a variety of ways to a variety of people.

Think box I

Try to brainstorm the number of support groups known to you.

In the *Think Box* above you might have mentioned:

- Addiction help (alcohol, drugs, gambling)
- Parenting groups
- Divorced people
- Anger management.

These groups are often unstructured, but equally often there is a designated leader. Many, if not all, of the dynamics we have studied so far will be observable in these groups, and it is perhaps artificial to separate a group from a team, at least as far as the dynamics are concerned. The chief difference is that a team will have a distinct *function* and will therefore be more task orientated than a group, where the purpose is achieved by membership itself and thus process is more important than content. A further difference is that a team will more often have a leader, whereas a group will either be unstructured or will have a facilitator who may well lead but whose function is rather different from that of a team leader. The importance of leadership in effective teamwork is crucial and often the success of a team in achieving its purpose or its task(s) can depend on the quality of its leader.

Below are the views of four healthcare team members about leaders and leadership (given specifically for this chapter):

'Leadership is about the relationship between the leader and the members of his or her team. It's made up of a whole range of methods, skills and characteristics. I don't think it's reasonable to expect all leaders to have some special charisma or to be inspirational, but they have to be able to provide whatever a team needs in terms of leadership. For many of the team, it's about the leader being able to protect the members' interests or acting on their behalf.'

'I believe that to be successful, a leader must above all be able to motivate the team — without that, success just isn't possible. To motivate, the leader has to give a lot. The leader has to earn respect, trust and loyalty from members and be able to back them up if things don't go well. Some people might say that when things are going well, leadership isn't too difficult, but it's when things go pear shaped that you can see whether a leader really is one.'

'For me, a leader has to set an example. They have to be good at their own job — I'm not saying that they have to be experts at everything in palliative care, but the team members need to know that the leader has...what do you call it... a good track record so that she or he can be a resource in the team. I have to say that some of the less than good team leaders I've had here haven't been too good at their jobs, either. If you don't have that sort of competence, I don't see, really, how you can lead anybody else.'

'It's difficult to define exactly what makes a leader. I'm not sure it's any one thing. I think to be a really good leader you have to have something a bit "different" about you. Perhaps it's something in the personality that goes along with being successful in their own field that sets them apart. (Although it's fair to say that plenty of people who are successful in that way don't always make good leaders.) With some people it's their way of communicating that does the trick, with others it's more their drive that lets them carry members along with them.'

You might have thought that effective leadership has something to do with achieving commitment and co-operation from all members and is based on trust

---

Think Box 2

From your own experience what do you think makes for good team leadership? Is it present in your care team?

---

and respect, that it is about ensuring that the diverse abilities within the team are used to maximum effect, that the whole is greater than the sum of its parts. Research (Handy, 2004) seems to show that what effective leadership is not about is the domination of the team by one person — however charismatic or competent she or he might be.

Dominant leaders seem to be unacceptable in situations where individuals have a free choice and are at best only tolerated in what we might call 'forced' situations, that is situations where members' jobs or prospects might be at risk if there is non-compliance with the leader.

This is what a practice nurse said regarding team leaders when interviewed for this book:

'In my previous job we had a very good team leader. I'm not sure how she did it, but she seemed to take account of everyone's opinions and suggestions and we always ended up more or less agreeing about the way forward. And she inspired quite a few of us, me included, to go on to further training, which I hadn't really had the confidence to do before. Now I find myself in a team where the leader makes all the decisions. So-called team meetings seem like a waste of time, because she doesn't really listen or take on board any one else's views. Don't get me wrong — a lot of what she makes us do is very good, but it's her way, not the team's. I love this job and I want to stay in it, but I don't really feel that I can make any worthwhile contribution to the team, only to the patients. I did try, but I felt a bit...demeaned, I suppose, as if my input was a bit tiresome or a waste of time, so now I don't bother. At least it means that meetings are quick!'

Think Box 3

Whether you yourself are a leader (or may in the future be one), or a team member, the role of the leader will have a strong effect on the ethos of the team to which you belong. Try to encapsulate the effect on team spirit of the leader(s) of the care teams to which you currently belong, or have been a member of in the past.

Perhaps you would agree that a team leader has three key areas of responsibility, as we mentioned for team models in chapter 2, and it is interesting that team responsibilities and leader responsibilities could be said to be the same (see *Figure 1*).

Figure 1. Team and leader responsibilities

    The three are closely inter-connected, and managing them depends to a great extent on the leader's style. Various writers have offered definitions of leadership style, but of course the diversity of styles cannot be wholly covered because the personality of leaders varies so greatly, and also a style appropriate for leading one team might be changed for a different set of members or a different task.

    One definition of leadership styles is that of Benson (1987). He suggests four possibilities:

- Directive
- Permissive
- Flexible
- Facilitative.

    The **directive** team leader is one who takes overall responsibility for the team's organisation, its tasks and goals. The **permissive** leader, on the other hand, works on the basis that members of the team are capable of making their own decisions and of coming to some sort of consensus with minimal direction. As the name suggests, the **flexible** leader is adaptable and will change his or her style to accommodate the needs of individual members and of the team itself. A **facilitative** leader sees him — or herself — both as a member of the team and as the person who has the knowledge and skills to keep the team functioning. You can perhaps see that content and process are involved here.

Think box 4

Which style of leadership might suit the following teams — all involved in hospice work?

A fundraising team
A team devising an in-service education programme
A team tasked with co-ordinating the hospice shops
A team trying to get validation for some of the hospice training courses
A team researching how to move to bigger/better accommodation
A team hoping to set up a bereavement support group

Research like Benson's has led to attempts to devise a 'leadership personality' profile by which leaders could be selected. However more recent research (Handy, 2004) seems to show that the personality of the leader is only one variable in predicting team effectiveness; what seems to matter is that leaders should be aware of their own style(s) and be able to consciously to select and adopt the right style for the right purpose. Look again at *Figure 1* illustrating the three key areas of responsibility; leadership style will reflect the relative importance each has for a leader. Perhaps even more important are the values and beliefs a leader holds about what constitutes a good organisation, a good member of that organisation, a good team and a worthwhile purpose, including which of the three areas is deemed to matter most.

Handy (2004) suggests that it is possible to develop the need for awareness about leadership style and that this will enhance team effectiveness (see *Activity 1*). The following exercise has been adapted from some of his suggestions.

It seems clear that leadership style must be appropriate to current

Activity 1

For the questionnaire below, look at the three statements in each of the five categories, and then give a ranking to each in the order which most closely represents your own personal beliefs and values (1 against the one which best fits your view, 2 against the next nearest, etc.). Add up all the scores for all the statements marked (a). Repeat for all the statements marked (b), then (c), etc. The lower the total score, the closer the statements are to your beliefs and values. Since some of the statements may not resonate exactly with your views, just try to follow your intuition. (*Continued overleaf*)

A good leader	Ranking (1 to 3)
(a) is impersonal and correct, avoiding the exercise of authority for own advantage	
(b) treats others as equals and is open to ideas concerning the task	
(c) is concerned and responsive to the personal needs and values of others	
A good manager	
(a) demands from staff only what is required by the formal system	
(b) uses authority to obtain the resources needed to get on with the job	
(c) uses position to provide stimulating work and development opportunities for staff	
A good team member	
(a) is responsible and reliable, meeting the duties and responsibilites of the job and avoiding actions which surprise or embarrass the manager or leader	
(b) is self-motivated to contribute to the task, is open to ideas and suggestions, but is also willing to give the lead to others when they show greater expertise or ability	
(c) is vitally interested in the development of own potentialities, is open to learning and receiving help, and respects the need to value others	
People are controlled and influenced by	
(a) impersonal exercise of power to enforce procedures and standards of performance	
(b) communication and discussion of task requirements by all team members	
(c) intrinsic interest and enjoyment	
It is legitimate for one person to control another's activities if	
(a) the role prescribes responsibility for directing the other	
(b) the person has more knowledge relevant to the task	
(c) the person is accepted by those who are controlled	

The results of this questionnaire will not be precisely accurate, but your rankings will give you a good indication of the direction you lean towards:

A low score for a: task orientated indicates a liking for lines of responsibility to be very clearly defined. The leader tends to agree, and then follow, procedures and expects the team members to do the same. There is very little spontaneity as matters are approached in a logical, analytical and methodical fashion. Knowledge and skill are valued. This style of leadership often leads to setting up of systems — perhaps for training or for appraisal of how the team is progressing towards achieving its task(s).

A low score for b: team orientated probably means that the leader believes in the team focusing in common on the task or problem. The ability to work co-operatively is extremely important and team members who are able to facilitate the work of the team as a whole are valued. The leader with this style sees members as resourceful human beings, rather than as human resources (it is interesting to speculate how this term came to replace the now rather old fashioned 'personnel'!). Roles and responsibilities for each team member are negotiated and agreed, rather than being decided by the leader or on the basis of status or perceived expertise. Self-development of individuals is encouraged. This last aspect of the style overlaps with the promotion of training in style (a), but here is more member- than leader-motivated.

A low score for c: individual orientated indicates that the leader tends to interact individually with members on a one-to-one basis. Full team meetings tend to be called and used only for the giving of information or to ask for suggestions or ideas. The leader values personal freedom and so encourages members to grasp any opportunities to develop themselves and the ways in which they work. Individual opinions and views are carefully listened to, valued and respected, even when they are not always part of a consensus of the team's views. The task is often used as a vehicle for developing individuals.

Each of these styles relates to the three areas in *Figure 1*.

Looking back at each of these styles, try to suggest an occasion in your healthcare team when each style might be appropriate. Are there any drawbacks if a leader adopts this style? What might they be? How might they be handled?

circumstances. Just as the team dynamic is not static, so the leader's style should not be stuck in one mode. If it is, there is a danger that the task, individuals or the team itself may suffer. A new manager of a community organisation said, in an interview for this chapter:

'I came from a business background and I think I saw myself as "leading from the front" — it probably worked because we got very good business results and either met or exceeded our targets. I thought it would be the same here and I came in with lots of ideas and was very keen to motivate people (the core team of employed staff and the volunteers) and I couldn't really understand why I didn't seem to be carrying everyone with me; it came as a bit of a shock really, because I'd always been able to do it before. I suppose I got a bit impatient — with myself as much as with anyone else. My self-belief was taking quite a knock when I realised that the team was just not functioning and I just couldn't seem to work out why. I remember making the excuse to myself that they just didn't like change! Then a friend took me aside and pointed out that palliative care concerns are rather different from business concerns (although in fairness to myself I'd say that they do have some things in common) and that there are different beliefs underpinning the work. He suggested that maybe a different style of leadership was called for. I thought it was worth a try (you can see that I don't like to fail!), and now I would say that I lead from the back rather than from the front. The work seems to get done and certainly the team seem much more co-operative and everyone gives more. I wish I had had more self awareness about how my style — I mean the style rather than me — was affecting things. Ah well, at least it seems to be going alright now, but the experience has taught me a lot about leadership.'

Here are five of the attributes which research has suggested a leader needs in order to build and sustain a successful and effective team:

- Feel personally responsible for the 'resources' involved (material, financial and, above all, human)
- Actively set out the direction the team is to take and accept the risks that this may involve (e.g. of challenge to his/her leadership)
- Communicate the direction/focus of the team and its objectives clearly, and inform of any changes or new information that may be relevant to fulfilling the objectives
- Maintain high standards of his or her own performance in order to model the standard expected of the whole team
- Be able to use the most appropriate leadership style for the individuals involved in the team and for the task.

Think box 5

Would you see these attributes as a good measure for leadership? Would you want to add anything? How does your own leadership or your team leader measure up on a scale of 1 to 6?

The qualities of a leader will underpin the functions a leader needs to perform in order that the team achieves its purpose and goals and that individual members are able to contribute to team success. A way of describing these functions is:

- **Initiating:** getting the work of the team going and keeping it moving along
- **Regulating:** influencing the direction, tempo or pace of the team's work
- **Informing:** bringing information or ideas to the team
- **Supporting:** creating an emotional climate which makes it easy for members to contribute and which holds the team together
- **Evaluating:** helping the team to appraise its decisions, goals, procedures and itself.

All five functions are crucial for cohesiveness (one of the essential features we noted earlier). Initiating is very important in the early stages of a team's work. Regulating and informing become increasingly important as the work progresses. Evaluating is important both at various stages of the work and at the end. Supporting functions are needed throughout.

Think box 6

Take a moment to consider how well (on a scale of 1–6) you, if you are a team leader, or your current leader, are carrying out these functions.

Initiating
Regulating
Informing
Supporting
Evaluating

It might be interesting to score members on a similar scale as role responsibility may mean that functions are not solely those of the team leader but are shared by team members, even if they are not shared equally.

A key way for team leaders to get the most out of themselves and out of the team is by **delegation.**

Leaders who delegate are demonstrating that they have full confidence in their team to work independently and believe that they can and will take responsibility for the task and for themselves.

There may be various reasons why a leader may not delegate and these are sometimes related to style. Some reasons are that the leader might have very little confidence in the members of the team; this can happen if the leader had no part in team selection. As one carers' support team leader expressed it:

'The individuals were just foisted on me, probably because they didn't fit in anywhere else, and I can tell you that for some time I just didn't dare to delegate.'

Another reason is that the balance of expertise among the members may be uneven and the leader becomes wary of asking anyone to do anything for fear of offending someone else! A few leaders will not delegate because they feel threatened by some (or all) of the team members and are fearful that they will be overtaken or made to look less competent than the people they are supposed to lead. Delegation can take up time initially but in the longer term it saves time and encourages full team input. Team leaders who are good delegators seem able to :

- Select members who are right for the particular task
- Ensure that those involved are able to see the task as an opportunity to enhance their own learning and development
- Take a back seat, yet at the same time be available for questioning and clarifying, especially if problems arise
- Agree what meetings are needed for reviewing progress
- Give individuals responsibility for their own part in the overall scheme and show trust in their ability to carry it out.

Think box 7

Think about the following in regard to your healthcare team:
    What is delegated?
    What could be delegated but currently isn't?
    Why is this not delegated?

Below is a list (not in any particular order) of the qualities of an effective leader, which summarises the points made in this chapter. The points were gathered from interviews with and letters from members of palliative care teams. An effective team leader:

- Has a clear vision about the short and the long-term purpose and objectives for the team
- Creates a sense of value and purpose in the work at hand, so that team members believe in what they do and strive to do it well
- Provides a positive sense of direction
- Acts decisively, but checks that the decisions are firmly based on team consensus
- Delegates some of the tasks, but doesn't keep checking and also does his or her fair share
- Sets the right tone based on beliefs, values and actions
- Provides enthusiasm
- Is available
- Is a good listener (but doesn't try to be the team counsellor or therapist!)
- Verbalises trust and respect
- Is sensitive to the expectations and needs of individual members
- Gives honest, frequent feedback, and knows that feedback is different from praise or criticism
- Defines responsibilities clearly and sees where there are limits
- Does not try to restrict the individuals or the team, but understands about boundaries
- Finds opportunities for all members to develop
- Admits own mistakes and tries not to make a moral issue of anyone else's mistakes
- Tries to develop loyalty and team spirit.

This is quite a tall order, yet it highlights what people want and expect from an effective leader.

Think box 8

As a final exercise go through the list above again and try to rank the qualities in the order they are most important to you, then identify three points which you think you as a leader, or a leader known to you in health care, have as particular strengths. Do the same for three points which could be improved. Reflect on how leadership affects your team.

Handy C (2004) *Gods of Management*. Heinneman, London

CHAPTER 7

Obstacles and ways of overcoming them

Although the power which a team generates can be several times greater than the power of each individual working 'solo', it is probably inevitable that from time to time the dynamic (as opposed to the task) will throw up problems. In this short final chapter we consider some of the possible obstacles to team working and reflect on how they might be overcome.

Teams are often so focused on the task that they never consider the process that they are using. Or, conversely, they are so focused on the inter-relationships within the team that they lose sight of the task — which can be very difficult if there are deadlines to be met and can also lead to over-hasty decisions. Highly effective teams need to balance the two. Some understanding of team roles and team roles theory can help to prevent an imbalance. When a team is formed, it is therefore useful to consider not only the expertise of individual members, important though this is, but also to consider how the type of role the member adopts will affect a team's dynamic.

There exists a term, *groupthink*, which is used to describe the situation when team members are too 'nice' to disagree with each other. Discussion then becomes very bland, and the diversity of opinion and varied input which ought to be one of a team's strengths is lost. Conflict need not be destructive; constructive dissent can only occur when team members feel safe enough to voice opinions or make suggestions that they know will not be met with hostility. The leader and team members can help to avoid groupthink by actively encouraging open discussion or debate and by ensuring that team members who seem to be holding back are deliberately asked to speak up. 'Groupthink' was very evident in a team of carers I spoke with. As one member put it:

'It was as if because carers are assumed to be nice people we were all afraid of offending each other if we said anything. I wanted to argue about the way the transport system for patients worked — I think I had some really good ideas for improving it, but I knew it was —'s "baby", so I never said anything. Now we're still using the same old system and I feel guilty because the patients aren't getting the best deal'.

The example shows that not only was the team not working as a team, but the task (of helping patients) was not being achieved either, because members were too concerned with being 'nice' to each other.

Think box 1

Consider the scenario described above. How could this situation be helped? Whose responsibility is it to change things?

Teams sometimes have difficult decisions to make. An effective and mature team will tussle with the problem and eventually reach a consensus. A less self-confident team may off-load the decision-making onto the leader, which is contrary to the whole point of having a team. A strong leader will refuse to be pushed into accepting responsibility and will urge the team to take responsibility for itself. This might involve encouraging members to continue working with the issue until some sort of consensus emerges, perhaps by focusing the team on moving forward rather than focusing on differences, if that is what is happening, and by reviewing points where there is already agreement and re-stating the team's goals. In terms of dynamics, the team might be encouraged to check whether all members have contributed or whether more vocal members are dominating. Consider the scenario below:

A hospice education team, which included a counsellor, social worker, some nurses, a fundraiser and the financial manager acting as team leader, were tasked with trying to decide whether study days should be continued as they were currently running at a loss. Part of palliative care's 'mission' is to educate and there was general agreement that this is desirable, but there was a range of views from individual members. Some members thought that the cost should be increased, but this was not acceptable to others, who thought that as far as possible study days should be 'open access'. The fundraiser representative was quite distressed to think that money which had been worked hard for should be spent on training rather than on patients; this provoked some discussion as to whether educating the public was, in various ways, actually benefiting patients. Some of the discussion was diverted by three members into what the syllabus for study days should be. The financial manager tried several times to point out that the books have to balance, and that a decision as to whether study days could be made to break-even, or whether they should close, was needed. Eventually, the team more-or-less told him that if those were the only alternatives and if that was the case, then he must take the decision to stop any more study days.

Think box 2

If you had been the team leader here, how might you have dealt with the decision making? If you had been a member of the team, would you have been satisfied with this outcome?

This scenario demonstrates how important it is for members to accept joint responsibility if they are to operate as a team. Even if decisions are difficult or unpopular there is less chance of a blame culture developing if the decision has been reached collectively, even if (for some members) reluctantly. Team spirit and ethos should generate give-and-take and mutual respect that the views of others are as important to them as yours are to you, so to speak. A supportive environment should ensure that disagreements are seen as healthy and are not a cause of (or excuse for) fight or flight.

Effective teams tend to be proactive; that is, they anticipate what needs to be done and make moves to achieve change or to implement an initiative. When pressured or if lacking in confidence, a team may become **reactive**; that is, they often put off decision-making until there is a crisis, almost as if there is some sort of belief that if things are ignored they will somehow go away. Teams which have been together for some time can also drift into a state of stasis where very little is achieved, or even become very resistant to change on the basis that *'we've always done it this way'*. The reactive team tends to lack energy and so when a problem occurs they resort to crisis management.

Sometimes the problem can be helped by the introduction of new members, although this may be initially resented. Sometimes the team needs to review itself and to be clear about its purpose. If it has genuinely outrun its life, then a decision about how to bring about the ending is needed. You will recall that Tuckman's model of a team's life has four stages. Some writers have proposed a fifth stage, variously called 'closure' or 'mourning'. Some groups close quite naturally because their task had been completed or achieved and this may not result in any strong features of sadness. Occasionally teams break up in disarray for a variety of reasons suggesting that the dynamic was never right in the first place. Sometimes there is genuine sadness when a team closes, and this is more likely if individuals have gained personal satisfaction and feel that team spirit has been a very positive experience. Consider the following scenario:

'A hospice bereavement support group had been meeting for several months. It was co-led by the counsellor and by one of the hospice chaplains and was 'closed' in the sense that after the first meeting there would be no new members. This had worked well and the group seemed effective in helping each other's grief — which was their purpose and the reason for the group's existence. After some time, the

leaders began to feel that the group was moving away from its task and that fewer and fewer members were talking about their grief or about bereavement. The members began to talk much more about meeting for social events and one or two actually took place. Whilst the leaders appreciated the need of the bereaved for social contact and were glad that members felt sufficiently confident to organise themselves to take part in activities, they were concerned that the purpose had been lost. In addition, they had sufficient bereaved people to start a new group and needed time and accommodation for them. Closing the group was a painful process, not least because it involved loss, which was not easy for the group members already experiencing loss. As a result of this experience they set much firmer ground rules and time boundaries for all future groups. They also reported that they used the experience to introduce firmer boundaries into the other teams with which they were involved in their work in the hospice.'

Think box 3

How important do you think ground rules are for team work? How do they contribute to the dynamic? How formal should they be?

Obstacles and difficulties will vary from team to team, but below are some possibilities:

- The composition of the team in terms of a balance of skills and expertise
- Problems with roles
- Communication within the team
- The atmosphere and ethos within the team
- The degree of member commitment
- Conflict between individual and team goals
- The clarity of purpose – members may not be clear about what they are trying to achieve and why
- The quality of leadership
- Confusion about decision making.

Are any of these obstacles present in your palliative care? Is the team as effective as it could be? Is the list sufficient? Would it be more effective if some of these obstacles were removed, or overcome? Whose responsibility is it to overcome obstacles?

These possible problems or difficulties in a team will obviously affect the four main area of team dynamics which we identified earlier:

- Communication patterns
- Cohesiveness
- Social control
- Team ethos.

Perhaps you can categorise the problems above (or in your team, should any of them exist) into these four areas.

A healthcare team which had the courage to perform what it called a 'team audit' asked for help with identifying barriers which seemed to be blocking achievement. Each member was asked to fill in a chart anonymously. The results were then copied to all members so that the team could prioritise and work on solutions. The stumbling blocks which were identified were:

- A lack of clear management direction
- The rather rigid hierarchy of the organisation's structure (one respondent talked about a triumvirate!)
- Uncertainty about the organisation's future both in financial and caring policy terms
- Too uneven mix of skills and expertise
- Low levels of motivation and commitment except to patient care
- Poor communication, leading to suspicion of secrecy and lack of trust.

Teamwork cannot solve every problem, but if problems are not identified then ways of working round or through them cannot happen. It is also often the case that 'small wheels will turn bigger wheels'. In the team above, clarity about the management's direction immediately helped with uncertainty about the future and improved motivation and general job satisfaction. This kind of team appraisal will often throw up complaints about the way individuals behave in the team. Teams can certainly benefit from self-diagnosis or review, but it is essential to be aware that the purpose is to enhance the team dynamic and not to engage in a sort of group moan. Coping with team members who seem to create difficulties is a team and not solely the task of the team leader.

Here are some of the difficulties complained about in a hospital team, with some suggestions as to how a responsible team might help to overcome them. As with the previous exercise, the complaints were given anonymously and in confidence, but a truly mature team should probably deal with them more openly.

1. The monopoliser
2. The silent, non-contributing member
3. The saboteur
4. The habitual joker
5. The 'know-it-all'

The monopoliser

Team control of a very talkative member for the sake of the overall team dynamic is a major challenge and has to be addressed in order to ensure that everyone who want to contribute gets a fair hearing. Useful phrases might be: *"I'm going to interrupt you, because I want to hear what *** has to say as I can see she's been trying to offer us something'*, *'What you've said is very helpful, but you don't have to carry everything — let us share the load'*. Judging the right time to intervene takes good observation skills and it is crucial that the would-be monopoliser is not made to feel that what they have said is not valued. Some ground rules, for example agreeing that everyone should have reasonable 'air time', can be very helpful. Commenting on how it is vital to respect the varied ways in which members may contribute can remind the talkative one about team process.

The silent non-contributing member

A silent, non-contributing member may not be speaking for a number of reasons: they are preoccupied; they lack confidence; they are bored (perhaps by the monopoliser!); they feel intimidated by others; they are reluctant members and do not feel that they belong, etc. It can be helpful to do some group exploration of who is feeling what in order to determine why there is silence and, if it has something to do with 'flight' then some work on team process is called for.

The saboteur

The saboteur is, for example, someone who habitually turns up late for team meetings or a member who persistently criticises ideas or suggestions without offering constructive alternatives. This person would need reminding what a team is. Pointing out the effect the sabotage is having on the team takes a deal of courage, but if done as part of understanding process it can improve the dynamic.

The habitual joker

Someone who seems intent on being a clown needs help, as this particular behaviour can distract the team from its purpose. A polite request to explain how the habitual joking is intended to help process will often lead to greater self–awareness and responsibility to the team. Humour is an excellent attribute in a team, but one member's habitual clowning is a distraction.

The 'know-it-all'

The 'know-it-all' is a serious danger to team dynamics as the other members can opt out (flight) and let him or her do all the work. Good listening and observation skills will help to identify triggers which can be challenged or worked round. For example: *'We know that *** knows a great deal about this, but I think we ought all to say something, so that any decisions aren't his alone'*.

We have mentioned ground rules as an aid to a healthy dynamic within a team. One palliative care organisation which covers a very large urban area of very mixed clientele and which offers both at-home and bedded support to end-of-life patients and their relatives and carers, decided to write a team working 'charter'. Since the staff and volunteers are so varied and, geographically, so widespread it was felt important to have a charter that all found acceptable. This is what the charter team proposed (see *Table 1*). When you have studied it, give your evaluation, and reflect on whether something similar would be of use to your own healthcare team.

Despite the problems highlighted in this chapter, it cannot be disputed that teams are an essential aspect of work and of health care in particular. If we are to fulfil the aim of providing holistic care of the highest quality, we perhaps owe it to those patients and to those nearest to them to understand something about the process of the team which aspires to fulfil that aim. We also owe it to ourselves and to our colleagues to appreciate the complexity of the dynamic in which we work, so that we can maintain and sustain the team.

As a final exercise try the quiz in *Activity* overleaf 1 to see how good your process skills now are:

Table 1 Team working charter

Establish clear aims	Intelligent groups can often find their own way if they know where to go People are often bogged down with methods
Start modestly	Success builds both confidence and further success People are more comfortable with concepts they can grasp
Ensure agreement before action	Commitment grows from real understanding Change without commitment is almost impossible Gaining commitment is time consuming
Build realistic time scales	Unlearning often needs to precede learning Cultural changes come slowly
Consult widely and genuinely	People do have valuable contributions to make Consultation increases commitment Consultation is not a chore, it is essential Manipulation undermines team building

Continued on next page

Relate team building to organisational work	Experimentation is more likely to be accepted if it does not involve substantial extra work Use regular meetings or projects as team building opportunities Meaningful results will be more easily identified
Face up to political problems	Do not sweep issues under the table Be realistic about what is attainable Playing politics will discredit your effort
Encourage openness and frankness	Deep-rooted prejudices and beliefs are more easily dealt with if discussed properly Do not stifle discussion
Do not raise false expectation	Promises are easy Broken promises discredit
Reorganise work if necessary	Developmental activities take time Team building can increase individual workloads
Remember that the unknown is often more threatening that the known	When problems are exposed they become less threatening
Remember that development is basically self-regulated	Age, capacity, and beliefs create limitations Ultimately, we are responsible for our own development
Remember that you can lead a horse to water but you cannot make it drink	People cannot be forced into attitude change People cannot be forced into openness and honesty People can be forced into pretending to change
Remember those who are not part of the action	Jealousy can develop People like to be part of the action
Remember that team building can precipitate other problems	Other groups can feel insecure Individuals and teams can grow beyond their present roles
Be open to other opportunities when team building	Individual development can occur New ideas generate further activity Challenges to existing systems and methods may present themselves
Delegate	People have different strengths ad skills Delegation usually mean development
Accept external help if necessary	Choose carefully Take responsibility for your own actions Outsiders offer different insights and skills Outsiders do not have organisational histories Outsiders are more likely to be impartial
Learn from mistakes	Admit when you are wrong Review progress regularly Encourage feedback Honest feedback is the most valuable thing your colleagues can give you
Practise what you preach	Actions speak louder than words

Activity I

Note whether you are doing 'all right', or would you like to 'do more' or ' do less' for each item below:

	Do more	All right	Do less
Communication skills Listening alertly Being brief and concise Drawing others out Keeping my remarks on the topic Thinking before I talk			
Observation skills Noting interest level in group Noting tension in the group Sensing feelings of individuals Noting who is being left out/ who is monopolizing Noting reactions to my comments Noting when a group avoids a topic Noting who talks to whom Noting how differences are being managed			
Self-disclosure Disagreeing openly Expressing warm feelings Being humorous Hiding emotions Telling others what I feel Being angry			
Tolerance to emotional situations Being able to: Face conflict and anger Face closeness and affection Face disappointment Stand silence Stand tension			
Social relationships Competing to outdo others Acting in a dominant way towards others Trusting others/ the group Being helpful Being protective Calling attention to myself Being able to stand up for myself Being open with others			

Source: National Extension College

Index